LEICESTER

and its Trams Tramscape and Townscape, 1903-1949

By Geoff Creese

IRWELL PRESS Ltd.

Copyright IRWELL PRESS LIMITED
ISBN 1-903266-68-8

First published in the United Kingdom in 2006
by Irwell Press Limited, 59A, High Street, Clophill,
Bedfordshire MK45 4BE
Printed by Newnorth Print, Bedford

Introduction

Horse-drawn trams commenced operation in Leicester in 1874 and lasted for thirty years before being superseded by electric trams. This new, clean, efficient and environmentally benign mode of transport was to serve Leicester faithfully for over 45 years before political considerations and replacement costs hastened the final closure of Leicester's tramway system, on 9 November 1949.

My original book, *Leicester's Trams* published in 2000 created much interest amongst the citizens of Leicester and indeed enthusiasts far beyond the city, so much so that the publishers have requested a second volume. In this I have been able to make use of further archive material, to slake the thirst for more of this specialised subject.

This further book focuses on trams in seldom-photographed locations and 'tramscapes' and where possible it avoids any repetition from the first book. The entire tramway era is covered and includes early horse-drawn scenes and views of 'The siege of Leicester' in 1903/4 when the trackwork being laid closed many main streets to traffic. The Clock Tower track layout, reputedly the most complicated ever laid in the British Isles, took just ten days to complete, largely by hand. A trade publication of 1904 comments that the quality of the trackwork, trams and material was 'unsurpassed' ... how true, as it largely remained untouched for over 45 years.

The visual evolution of the trams is depicted from the delivery of the original batches in open top form, followed by a batch with canopy roofs and the gradual modernisation of the entire fleet to the final 'enclosed' condition in which they were scrapped in favour of the diesel motor-bus, at a fraction of the cost of new trams.

A deficiency of the original book was the absence of photographs of the sole survivor, Tram No.76, in service, and its later restoration to 1920s condition in which it is exhibited at the Tramway Museum at Crich, near Matlock, Derbyshire. A short section on its life and times will I hope 'get me off the hook'.

No tramway system could function without the staff, of all grades and skills. Few photographs exist of the workshops but I have included those suitable for reproduction as an insight into the machinery used in the early twentieth century and before 'Health and Safety' ruled all.

The Trams collected power from the overhead copper wire which spanned every route. This had to be well maintained and it is appropriate to include photographs of the 'Tower Wagons', both horse and motor powered, that were used to service the wires.

Fortunately the first motorised Tower Wagon, dating from 1911, has been preserved by The Leicester Museum of Technology, who have also created at the Abbey Pumping Station (itself a masterpiece of civic pride and Victorian engineering) an exhibition entitled 'A Tramsport of Delight'. This includes a recreated lower deck of a tram, photographs and archive material of great interest.

To experience the pleasure of tram riding, a visit to Crich near Matlock, Derbyshire is essential. The National Tramway Museum or 'Tramway Village' as it has become, celebrated its 50th anniversary in 2005 and from humble beginnings has developed into a world-renowned working tramway and museum, in the midst of glorious countryside. And, of course, it is the home of Leicester No.76.

This author was born and educated (at the 'Wyggeston') in Leicester and being 'of a certain age' has clear memories of the trams in their declining years. I also commenced my banking career in the city in the 'pen and ink' age when Bank Managers were pillars of society. Leicester's Trams are still remembered with affection and nostalgia and this further offering would not have been possible without encouragement, persuasion and help from many kind friends. To Glynn Wilton, the Curator at Crich Tramway Village; Stuart Warburton at The Abbey Pumping Station; BBC 'Radio Leicester' and the *Leicester Mercury*, also Peter Newland, a real expert on Leicester's Trams and Buses, my sincere thanks are due. I am very fortunate to have an outstanding publisher, who has been most

A 1903 view of the Clock Tower in the centre of Leicester, surrounded by new tram track being laid. The complex nature of the trackwork, supplied by Hadfields of Sheffield, is clearly evident. The narrow street ahead is Churchgate and one familiar name, Freeman Hardy and Willis, synonymous with boots and shoes, occupies the imposing building behind the Clock Tower.

supportive (and persuasive!). However without the foresight of the photographers of a bygone age none of this would have been recorded. While I pay tribute to all, may I mention just one ... Henry Priestley, born in the Edwardian era and still 'on track' who recorded tramways throughout the British Isles for posterity. I have treasured correspondence from this remarkable gentleman many of whose pictures are reproduced herein, with permission. For forty years my wife Anita has put up with my obsession with vintage transport and a nostalgic interest in Leicester as it was in my youth. During the compilation of this second book her patience and support has been unfailing as has that of my daughter Juliet, whose computer skills and help in preparation of the captions have been essential. Therefore to both my everlasting thanks and appreciation, I know it will cost...

On May 14 1949, the penultimate day of the East Park Road routes, Tram No.154 drifts down Evington Road before turning left into East Park Road, home to many well-known Leicester factories. Alongside No.154 is a late 1937 Morris 10 car, FMM341 registered in Middlesex, driven by a nervous 'Learner' driver, no doubt thinking it would be easier if the trams were withdrawn. In the background is a brand new 1949 AEC Regent III bus on Route 30 leading for Highway Road. It was one of a fleet of 160 new buses supplied by Leyland, AEC and Daimler to replace the trams, the basic design of which dated from 1904. National Tramway Museum.

TRAFFIC-FREE TOWN ROUTES

HOW TO BY-PASS THE BUSY THOROUGHFARES OF LEICESTER

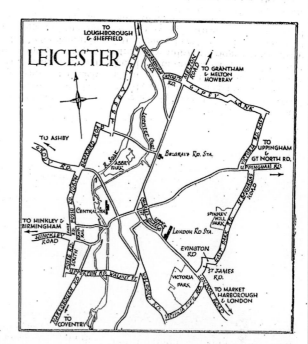

Map of Leicester showing the route and places referred to in this article.

MOTORISTS approaching Leicester from Market Harborough and London, and proceeding in the Uppingham Road direction, usually enter the town via London Road. After passing Victoria Park on the left look out for St. James Road, just beyond a church on the right. Turn down here, and continue to the cross-roads at Evington Road. At this point turn right and follow the tram-lines to the left, into East Park Road—a wide, straight thoroughfare which passes over several cross-roads, changes its name to St. Barnabas Road, and comes out at Uppingham Road, where a right-hand turn leads to Uppingham and the Great North Road.

Those proceeding towards Melton Road should turn left at Uppingham Road, and then take the second on the right—known as Victoria Road East. After about three-quarters of a mile this emerges at a " T "-shaped junction in Gipsy Lane. Here turn left, passing below the railway and keeping a general north-westerly direction, bearing left and right, to a wide crossing at Melton Road. At this point, turn right for Melton Mowbray and Grantham. Proceeding to Loughborough, cross over

Melton Road, go straight ahead up the incline, Checketts Road, and at the end bear right into Loughborough Road. After about 400 yards this joins Abbey Lane, where the direction posts show Loughborough quite clearly.

A Road to Watch For

Approaching from London Road and making for destinations west of Leicester, look out for an opening on the left of London Road—Victoria Park Road—just before reaching Victoria Park. Go along here, until you meet Welford Road; turn right and continue to the Rugby football ground. At the next fork, double back into Walnut Street, the fourth opening on the right. After two crossings, Walnut Street becomes Upperton Road, crosses the canal and the railway, and finally comes out at Narborough Road, where a left-hand turn leads to Coventry.

Proceeding in the Hinckley direction, motorists wishing to avoid the Braunston Gate-Narborough Road junction should continue along Upperton Road to Fosse Road South. There turn right, and then on reaching Hinckley Road turn left. For Ashby-de-la-Zouche carry on along the Fosse Road route, pass over Hinckley Road and continue in a northerly direction for about one mile, passing below the railway and coming to the junction of Groby Road and Wood Gate. Turn left along Groby Road for Ashby. To reach the exit for Sheffield, Loughborough and Buxton from this point, go straight ahead at the Groby Road crossing, into Blackbird Road. Turn right, at the top pass underneath a railway bridge, and take the first on the left—Abbey Lane —which ultimately merges into Loughborough Road.

Leicester is surrounded on the east by St. James Road, East Park Road and Victoria Road East; on the north by

Gipsy Lane, Checketts Road and part of Loughborough Road; on the south by Victoria Park Road, Walnut Street and Upperton Road ; and on the west by Fosse Road (North, Central and South), Blackbird Road and Abbey Lane. These routes form an almost complete by-pass round the town, so that, no matter from what direction one approaches Leicester, it is always possible to reach an exit road without passing through congested streets. For example, many owner-drivers from the Midlands want to avoid heavy traffic on their way to the Great North Road or places east thereof. Instead of the normal route through Braunston Gate, West Bridge, Nicholas Street, to the Clock Tower, and thence, via Humberstone Gate to Humberston Road and Uppingham Road, there is a traffic-free alternative in Upperton Road, Walnut Street, Victoria Park Road, St. James Road and East Park Road.

Avoiding Congested Areas

Again, motorists from the Loughborough direction, travelling towards Coventry or Birmingham, will avoid the congested main thoroughfares by using Abbey Lane, turning right at its junction with Blackbird Road and Abbey Park Road, and continuing to the left with Blackbird Road. Crossing over Groby Road into Fosse Road North, there is an ideal traffic-free route all the way along Fosse Road and Fosse Road South, at the end of which—just after the railway bridge—turn sharp left, coming to a " T "-shaped junction in Narborough Road. At this point turn right for Coventry.

From London Road to Belgrave Gate a new arterial road saves the busy motorist's time. This is a continuation of Charles Street and Upper Charles Street, and completely avoids all the congestion of Granby Street.

c5

One Leicester Tram has survived, No.76. The upper photograph was taken in 1938 at the Aylestone Terminus, by Henry Priestley. Headgear was mandatory in those long distant days. The public house was the "Rutland Arms", then a "Bass" house. No. 76 was built by Dick Kerr & Co. of Preston, in 1904, cost £510. During its working life of 43 years which ended in January 1948 its appearance was altered, like all Leicester trams, to the condition seen above. It was disposed of in 1948 to Edlins of Blaby, Leicester, who resold the body for use as a cricket pavilion! It was rediscovered in 1960 in South Yorkshire by a group of early members of the Tramway Museum, who raised the sum of £100 to purchase the body and transport it to Crich, Derbyshire. There followed many years of hard work by a dedicated group of enthusiasts, who located many missing parts and restored the tram to its 1920s condition (below). It is now on permanent display in the Exhibition hall at Crich, home of the National Tramway Museum.

Left. 'Hill Top' as the junction of London Road, Evington Road and Victoria Park Gates was originally known, on May 14 1949. Tram No.6, one of twenty-three rebuilt with lengthened (and strengthened) frames, begins to turn into Evington Road on the anti-clockwise Route 1 East Park Road circular. The original London Road Branch of Lloyds Bank is visible behind the tram. It is remembered by the author who began a banking career there in 1956. Road traffic is sparse even though it was a Saturday; an early post-war Ford Prefect appears to be keeping within the tram tracks, while a black Vauxhall 14 descends towards University Road. Leicester Photographic Society.

Below. Shortly before closure of the Clarendon Park Route, on 15 March 1949, Trams Nos.7 and 93 are passing each other on one of the many loops on this route, in this case near to the Knighton Library at the St Leonards Road Junction. Worthington's the grocers are on the left. K. Aldridge on the right was a local 'English and Foreign' fruiterer, next to Pell the Butcher (the white tiled shop) where sadly little meat is on display, due to shortages and rationing. Leicestershire Museums F.N.T., L.L. Jones.

On 14 May 1949 Tram No.7 negotiates the turn into Evington Road, while Tram No.102 follows on London Road, heading for Stoneygate, Route 3. Only two road vehicles are in sight, a Fordson lorry, identified by its utilitarian radiator, while parked in Granville Road to the left is a 1938 Morris 8.

The photographer positioned himself in Shanklin Drive, Stoneygate to take this view of No.36 on a special tour of the system, organised by the 'Southern Counties Touring Society' on 8 May 1949. The enthusiasts are not of the trainspotter variety but appear to be middle-aged men, in their gabardine raincoats. In the bay window (upper deck) is a young lady; no doubt her husband was a tram 'nut'. On the far left a Transport Inspector is supervising the 'capped' gentleman, manhandling the trolley by using the bamboo pole carried on all Leicester trams. Not an easy task. The end of the line was only 200 yards to the right, on London Road, and an automatic trolley reverser was a standard installation. This 'treat' was no doubt for the enthusiasts' benefit. After closure of the system No.36 (bearing advertisements for 'Schweppes' mineral waters and Kirby and West Dairies) was earmarked for preservation by Leicester Museum but it was not to be. However, Schweppes and Kirby and West survive to this day. What a pity the tram did not. Leicestershire Museums F.N.T., L.L. Jones.

In December 1948 No.136 runs through a typical tramscape near to the Highcross Street, Sanvey Gate and Soar Lane junction on route 9, heading for Groby Road. While the tramway appears to be still in good repair, the 1935 Austin 'Lichfield' 10hp car JF 8650 would have rattled and creaked as it rumbled along following the tramlines. Awaiting the opportunity to leave Sanvey Gate is a c.1942 Midland Red double deck bus with a utility body. Thankfully Gilbey's Gin is still with us!

In January 1949 Tram No.173 is leaving Victoria Park Road to enter Queens Road, heading for Clarendon Park, Route 4. The conductor has been rather presumptuous, changing the destination blind to 'Blackbird Road' at this point of the outward bound journey and over a mile from the terminus. On the left in the Victoria Park grounds can be seen the World War Two Nissen huts occupied by the RAOC/RASC pay departments and not removed until well into the 1950s. Pearce & Son Ltd jeweller's in the Market Place occupied what was the oldest shop in the city, dating from 1597. Leicestershire Museums F.N.T., L.L. Jones.

The end of the line at Stoneygate Terminus in 1947. This trio of trams has not arrived simultaneously as No.138 is on a 'Special' touring the surviving routes with a group of Light Railway Transport League members. No.138 will reverse and cross over to the city-bound tracks, allowing No.51 and later No.37 (both on the Stoneygate service) to follow and maintain the normal schedule of a tram every three minutes. Grenfell Road can be seen on the right and the waybill checker (which had to be used by each conductor to record the departure time, hopefully in accord with the timetable) is on the left. National Tramway Museum.

A busy scene at the Clock Tower in April 1949 with Tram No.109 (one of a batch with a canopy domed roof from new in 1905) has travelled from the Abbey Park Road Depot and is turning into Humberstone Gate to take up duty on the Humberstone Route, No.8. The Dodge Lorry, DJF 286 dating from 1946, is followed by a new Austin A40 van, FJF 474. Both are registered in Leicester. The Clock Tower is surrounded by scaffolding for periodical maintenance purposes and the fashions worn by the pedestrians are a far cry from the casual and sloppy dress of today. Leicestershire Museums F.N.T., L.L. Jones.

Mayfield Road, London Road and Victoria Park Road form this junction as Tram No.9 turns into the latter on Route 4 Clarendon Park. The solitary motor car is a 1948 Alvis TA14, a luxury car. Part of St James the Greater Church can just be seen in this picture taken prior to March 1949. Leicestershire Museums F.N.T., L.L. Jones.

In early 1949 Tram No.56 is entering St Barnabas Road from Uppingham Road where a young lady, typically wearing a headscarf on a windy day, awaits by the 'Belisha Beacon', either to board the already well-loaded tram, or to cross the road. Route No.2 East Park Road circular was the clockwise service via Humberstone Road, Uppingham Road, St Barnabas Road, East Park Road and Evington Road before heading down London Road to the Clock Tower. Goodwin's 'Extra' self raising flour, presumably was of superior quality than some of its competitors. Leicestershire Museums F.N.T., L.L. Jones.

Melton Turn, on a sunny day in June 1948 with a well-groomed No.58 heading out of Loughborough Road and definitely NOT keeping left of the bollards! The Westminster Bank became Nat West (National Provincial and the Westminster Bank amalgamated); Bacon's Garage advertises wedding cars, and is an agent for Pole's Luxury Coaches. Notwithstanding the variety of petrol pump globes indicating 'Dominion', 'Carless' (an odd name for a petrol company when you think about it) and 'Shell' petrols, it was all the same appalling 'Pool' petrol at this period. The Mechanical Horse following the tram is a 'Karrier Scammell' three wheeler and trailer favoured by the LMS Railway for local deliveries. Tram No.58 was to achieve 'stardom' as the last to run in Leicester, on 9 November 1949 when the system closed for good. Leicestershire Museums F.N.T., L.L. Jones.

In early 1946 Tram No.46 is heading along Granby Street on Route 1 East Park Road. The scene is drab and with only one car, a Vauxhall 25hp, ANR 159 registered in August 1937; austerity is the watchword. On the left a news vendor stands selling the 'Evening Mail' or the 'Leicester Mercury'. On the left-hand corner of Bishop Street stands the Midland Bank (now HSBC) and the 'Picture House' is sandwiched between the Midland and its competitor, the National Provincial Bank. As befits a city known for boots and shoes, the shopper is spoilt for choice, with Dolcis and Freeman Hardy & Willis and, beyond, Pochin's Hardware, and the Turkey Café and Briggs Shoes.

On 28 January 1939 Eastgates and High Street, notwithstanding the weather, are filled with trams. No.144 is identifiable and, bearing no adverts, is destined for Route 2, Narborough Road. Traffic is sparse with a Hillman Minx of 1933 vintage parked alongside the two trams and a two seater tourer with a 'dicky seat' (probably a late 1920s Morris) following No.144. Note the news vendor standing between the tracks; the studs indicated a pedestrian crossing. All the buildings still exist and the 'Great Sale' of Phillips (home furnishers) with its 'Lowest Cash Price' has a familiar ring to it. 'British Home Stores' catered for all tastes with goods priced from 3d to 5/- (25p).

Tram No.138 about 1905 on Hinckley Road heading for Western Park. It is 'as built' by Dick-Kerr of Preston, i.e. open-topped, with the ladies in their finery and children dressed in their Sunday best. A church on the right adds to this peaceful scene on a perfect day. The tram cost £510 when new and certainly provided value for money through a working life of 45 years.

Victoria Park Road showing the Army Nissen huts in the park behind the wooden fencing. Tram No.7 is approaching, on its way to Clarendon Park in the winter of 1948/49 bearing an advert for 'Cephos' the Physician's Remedy for Headaches and Neuralgia... Long deleted, no doubt, from the apothecary's almanac!

A variety of transport on 16 December 1948 at the Blackbird Road, Groby Road, Woodgate junction. Trams Nos.70 and 150 are on the Blackbird Road reservation opened in 1924 for the Royal Show, while a solitary cyclist and pedestrian (ladies of course!) risk their lives as an elderly LCT Bus No.261 and an American Ford Utility Wagon approach. The road signs are of a style long gone and at the date of the photograph the 'arrow' sign 'LNER Station - Leicester Central' was obsolete, for the railways had been nationalised on 1 January 1948. A.D. Packer.

'The Hole on the Wall' in Humberstone Gate, the entrance to the depot next to the *Bell Hotel*, gave no indication as to its interior, shown here on 8 May 1949 housing a number of 'off duty' trams. The tram enthusiasts were members of the Southern Counties Touring Society who had No.36 on which to tour the system. On the floor lies a point change key. National Tramway Museum.

Tram No.7 at the Shanklin Drive corner on 8 May 1949, approaching the Stoneygate Terminus with the destination blinds already changed for the return journey to Belgrave. Tram No.36 is full of enthusiasts on a Southern Counties Touring Society visit to the remnants of the system. After this the car was little used as it was earmarked for preservation – as we have seen, sadly No.36 was nonetheless broken up on 24 April 1950. National Tramway Museum.

Tram No.36 going uphill on Evington Road, leading to Victoria Park and London Road while on an enthusiasts special, 8 May 1949. The passing loop is in the foreground and the tracks and setts appear to be in satisfactory condition. Nevertheless, one week later the route was closed and the trackwork simply tarmaced over. Even today in some parts of the city the tram tracks are still there, under several layers of the black stuff. Kirby & West, 'Leicester's Leading Dairy' is still just that, 56 years on. Long may it remain so. National Tramway Museum.

Initially the tramways employed 'pointsboys' particularly around the complex trackwork surrounding the Clock Tower. In 1905 these four lads pose outside a wooden shelter, no doubt proud to have a job – and free uniform! The oil-filled lamps would have been used at night or in foggy weather to indicate to tram drivers whether it was safe to proceed. Peter Newland.

In April 1947 Tram No.118 approaches the city centre with Woolworths and the 'Zip' dry cleaners on the left. Turner Jacques – high class gent's outfitters – is on the corner of Halford Street. The National Provincial Bank stands proudly on the corner of Horsefair Street displaying a banner for 'Defence Bonds' a safe and secure government investment bearing interest at 2½% gross! Apart from the LCT bus in the background, road traffic was conspicuous by its absence as petrol was unobtainable for private motoring. The US sponsored 'Marshall Aid' package formed the basis of our eventual survival and economic recovery.

Trams galore in High Street on a fine day in 1930. On the left are the new loading barriers for the Narborough Road and Western Park Routes, No.160 bearing the former destination. Route numbers had yet to be introduced. The premises of 'Hoggetts the Tailors' is prominent as is the neo-classical façade of Lloyds Bank on the right. John Manners, school outfitters, with the window blinds down, displays the badges of the four city grammar schools, most prominent of which is that of the Wyggeston, which the author attended in the 1950s. It is now a Sixth Form college, with a renowned tradition.

Photographs of trams on the Welford Road to Clarendon Park route, opened in 1922, are rare. However, on 16 July 1939 (a Sunday and a glorious day) Tram No.21 was on a Light Rail Transport League enthusiasts' tour of the system. The precise location is the Clarendon Park Road junction and the tram is stationary on Welford Road. Safety was not an issue judging from the upper deck with 'tramspotters' seemingly taking advantage of the fully open windows to get in the picture. At this date the houses were residential; now they are largely used for commercial purposes and the road is heavy with traffic, a contrast to this scene 66 years ago, with just one car in the distance. Travel Lens Photographic.

The Midland Railway station built in 1892 to the design of Charles Trubshaw is now Grade I listed and rightly so. In 1906 No.120, delivered in 1905 as one of the first tramcars with a canopy roof and partially enclosed, is heading for East Park Road, although the policeman appears to be in a vulnerable position. The solitary 'vehicle' in the scene is a horse-drawn wagon which may belong to the Midland Railway. The ornate gantries supporting the overhead wires are prominent; gas street lamps complete the scene.

Gallowtree Gate in October 1948 on a sunny day, No.156 heading for East Park Road on Route 1. Its paintwork is workstained as it is largely in pre-1935 livery though the driver's 'courtesy panel' has been repainted in maroon with the later style of plain numbering. 'Spalls' was a long-established gift shop; the otherwise anonymous shop is in fact Woolworths, no doubt undergoing a post-war refit. The solitary motor car is a 1935 Vauxhall 14.

Outside the 'Premier Works' on Melton Road in June 1948, Tram No.74 with a patched courtesy panel heads towards the Clock Tower and on to Humberstone passing No.66 heading for the Melton Road terminus. 'Kemdex' was a fixadent for dentures and 'Top Mill' was a brand of snuff. DJF12 is a Fordson 10hp milk van; the preceding car, in need of a new engine judging by the exhaust fumes, is a 1934 Standard. Leicestershire Museums F.N.T., L.L. Jones.

Granby Street in 1938. Tram No.100 heads towards the city centre from Stoneygate; it will proceed to Fosse Road on Route 3. An Austin 10 is parked in front of the National Cash Register Co Shop while an American 'Oldsmobile' is outside the 'Roneo' duplicator shop. Outside Russell's music and piano emporium is a Morris 10cwt van used by the LMS and LNE railways for local parcels deliveries, while approaching is a 1932 Morris Minor. Parked outside 'Harris of Granby Corner' is a 1936 Morris Commercial Van belonging to Leicester Co-operative Society. The traffic signs are simple and clear but Granby Street is now one way and all traffic veers to the right and on to a new flyover, avoiding much of central Leicester.

On Saturday 15 July 1947, Gallowtree Gate is alive with shoppers and the trams are still the principal mode of public transport. Nos.51 and 39 are heading towards the Clock Tower where they will turn left into Eastgates and the High Street loading barriers and on to Western Park on the Hinckley Road. The once famous 'Bovril' sign is visible beyond the Clock Tower; at this date the system was largely intact and the trams clean and well-maintained, providing an unsurpassed service to the public. Buses only operated (generally speaking) in areas not served by the trams.

In 1938 at the High Street/Highcross Street intersection, the now-preserved tram No.76, rarely photographed during its working life, is heading towards the Clock Tower and then Route 4 to Clarendon Park. It is in immaculate condition, as indeed was the entire fleet. It displays the additional destination board on the lower deck which often confused visitors to the city. The car is a 1937 Wolseley 14, a model much favoured by the Police for traffic duties. The Midland Bank on the corner is now a Bookmakers. National Tramway Museum, H.B. Priestley.

In 1938, on a dull day, No.53 turns into Woodgate heading towards the Clock Tower and then to Belgrave. Balfour Street is to the left of Tom Cann Ltd, a garage with two Austin 12s in the showroom. The line of petrol pumps at a small suburban garage is quite startling. The brands available have been identified left to right as ROP (Russian Oil Products), National Benzole, Power, Dominion, Shell and Redline Glico. With not a motorist in sight, the pump attendant is not surprisingly sitting down between the ROP and Nat. Benzole Pumps. A sole cyclist pedals nonchalantly by. In 2005, petrol stations and supermarkets offer no choice of brand and it is hard to appreciate that back then there really were six individual petrol tanks underground.

In 1913/14, twenty additional tramcars with longer frames and wheelbases were delivered for an experiment with 'PAYE'; not a tax collecting measure but 'Pay As You Enter'. It was an early but unsuccessful experiment to aid fare collection and speed passenger loading and unloading. The tram, No.148, is 'as delivered' with a platoon of staff on parade for what was an undoubtedly an official photograph.

A 1903 scene in Belgrave Gate. No trams but full of social history. Tracklaying was in progress with no mechanical aids in sight except, maybe, a wheelbarrow. This was a poor part of Leicester and the buildings even then were well past their prime. George Street (nowadays almost submerged by the Burleys flyover) displays adverts, sadly obscured, for a Health & Beauty soap and below, at a guess 'Mothaks' to destroy moths and beetles. The inevitable pawnbrokers is denoted by the three suspended balls on the left, opposite the *Rutland Arms*. Much of this area was cleared in the 1930s and is now totally unrecognisable.

Prior to the delivery in 1911 of the first Leyland lorry (BC 1078) for overhead wire maintenance, this horse-drawn Tower Wagon No.2 was used. The horses have been well groomed by the driver who sports a rosette. The cap worn by the man standing appears to read 'Overhead Superintendent' an important person whose assistant is sitting up front with the Driver. The lettering on the Tower Wagon itself indicates that T. Robert Smith was the Assistant Engineer and the legend reads 'Leicester Tramways'. The ensemble is in Bowling Green Street behind the Town Hall, about 1906. Peter Newland.

Shortly after the introduction of Route Numbers in 1932, Tram No.109 waits at Belgrave Terminus. It was one of a batch of twenty delivered from the makers, United Electric Car Co, with roofs noticeably more domed than the remainder of the fleet. The 'Gents' is a rather rudimentary structure, probably cast in iron, while the lady's cycle, complete with a chain oil bath, is being ridden well away from the tram lines. National Tramway Museum.

Gallowtree Gate on a dull day in May 1949, and No.118 approaches the Clock Tower junction, which it will cross into the Haymarket to unload passengers still on board from Stoneygate and embark fresh passengers for Belgrave. Not withdrawn until October 1949 its condition is far from pristine. The buildings still largely exist, although occupied by different retailers. The utility Bedford lorry, GJJ953 registered in London in 1941, is a reminder of the once-familiar parcel vans painted in the plain mid-green livery of Carter Patterson. This firm had a joint operation with Pickfords, the latter being well known for house removals and the movement by road of very large industrial loads. The driver's hand signal suggests that he is about to turn into Eastgates and High Street. National Tramway Museum.

No.118 is photographed later, on the same journey... Location Melton Turn... about to turn into Loughborough Road and Belgrave. The Allens bus, a "Leyland", dates from 1937 as does the impressive American "Studebaker" car, over taking the tram on the inside! One of the last trams to remain, its condition is far from pristine; the route closed on 9th October 1949. National Tramway Museum.

On a winter's day in 1927 Tram No.1, with part enclosure of the upper deck, has arrived at the Stoneygate Terminus; it will return to the Clock Tower and then on to Narborough Road. The setts indicate the entrance to the former Tram Shed, closed in 1924 and subsequently rented out to Messrs. H.A. Browett who traded as the 'Terminus Garage'. YM 759 is a 'Bullnose Morris' Cowley registered in London around 1926. Shell Petrol is well known but is it still 'guaranteed'? The petrol tank located in the bulkhead of the Morris was once a common – if alarming in retrospect – feature of early cars. The gentleman smartly attired in overcoat and wearing a trilby style hat is Mr Browett himself.

Melbourne Road was rarely photographed, for it was the first route to close, in December 1933. In 1907, Tram No.46 in its original open top condition is approaching a passing loop on the tree lined road lit by elegant gas lamps. By December 1933 the trackwork was life expired and the route was converted to bus operation.

A sad sight; No.15, stripped of all electrical and reusable fittings, on a low loader hauled by an American ex-military tractor, en route to Edlins of Blaby where it will be broken up. It still displays its last working destination, Aylestone, closed on 5 January 1947. No.15 was withdrawn just ten days later. The location is Welford Road near the junction with University Road. On the left are the Wyggeston Boys Grammar School playing fields and to the right, behind the youngster gazing in awe (surely) at No.15 are the Freeman's Common allotments. Although the track has been lifted on this short-lived Welford Road line to Clarendon Park (closed 1st May 1945) the overhead copper wire has yet to be reclaimed. Peter Newland.

The Clock Tower, the pivotal centre of Leicester, in July 1938. Tram No.107 displaying Route 4 – Clarendon Park – is keeping right to turn into Gallowtree Gate. The traffic policemen are wearing summer uniform, white helmets, armbands and gloves. Apart from the motor cycle and sidecar, the driver of which is wearing traditional 'leathers', the cars are all Fords. The Ford 8 of 1936 vintage is being driven by an 'L' driver, the test having been compulsory since June 1935. All the buildings behind the Clock Tower are long gone as the site has been redeveloped as the Haymarket Centre. The Refuge Assurance Co has been lost in the many take-overs in the insurance industry. The Fifty Shilling Tailor (£2.50p) was famed for cheap off the peg two piece suits for men, while Stones Television was probably one of the earliest TV retailers in the country. TV broadcasts commenced in 1936, BBC only. As is well known, the newsreaders (men only) wore dinner jackets when 'on air'. National Tramway Museum, W.A. Camwell.

London Road in the summer of 1904, shortly after opening. New No.21 heads for Stoneygate. The two policemen on duty stand astride the tramlines to the left. Their lot seems to be quite a happy one!

Three 'water cart' trams were operated and this picture of about 1906 in Granby Street is unique in showing No.100 (later No.179) at work spraying the tracks and setts with (probably) disinfectant. The Midland Bank is just visible on the corner of Bishop Street while to the right are R. Pochin & Son Ironmongers, hardware merchants who incidentally still exist a century later on, relocated to modern premises. Singer Sewing Machines shop is next door, adjacent to a tobacconist advertising 'Marshuma Cigars'. J. Herbert Marshall retailed pianos and organs and boasted a Music Gallery. Most buildings have survived, albeit with different occupants. The pedestrians are well dressed – Leicester was a prosperous manufacturing centre, after all.

Very few photographs exist of trams on the Clarendon Park via Welford Road line. However, in October 1937 No.23 is descending Cemetery (on left) Hill and crossing the LMS main line to St Pancras, city-bound to Horsefair Street. The tram stop on the right is in an isolated position, away from any housing; even boys from the Wyggeston School at the brow of the hill would have had a hike! Kirby & West thankfully is still the city's Leading Dairy and the scene is largely unaltered, other than by the removal of all reminders of the tramway era.

In Coronation year 1937 the bodies of two trams, Nos.29 and 24 withdrawn in 1933, serve as stores for the bunting and decorations used to adorn the trams that May. They show the partially enclosed upper decks, an intermediate stage in the piecemeal modernisation of Leicester Trams. The bodies still appear to be in sound condition and No.29 defiantly displays 'Melbourne Road'; this was the first route closed, in December 1933, hence their withdrawal. The depot 'GUY' lorry RY6754 dates from 1928.

On a grim and wet day in 1941, Trams Nos.95 (just repainted) and 17 (old livery) are both on the East Park Road circular routes, No.95 on Route 2 clockwise and No.17 on Route 1 anti-clockwise from the Clock Tower, turning from and to Evington Road at its junction with London Road. Salisbury Road is to the left. Lloyds Bank can be seen between the trams which have the wartime blackout fittings on the headlamps. This virtually obliterated any light, especially at night when you needed it.

As indicated several times throughout this text, Leicester's trams were always maintained to a very high standard hence their longevity. Pictured in the workshops in 1930, Tram No.146 is supported on lifting jacks as the wheelsets and axleboxes await attention. The workshop itself is a hive of activity with numerous skilled workers at their benches. Various parts are seen to the right, carefully grouped, with numerous wheelsets and main drive gears lined up over the pits.

Inside the depot in 1937, several trams and watercarts await their next duties. Only No.127 has been repainted in the simplified livery then recently introduced. The paintwork of the two watercarts No.179 on the left and No.180 in the right-hand corner is shabby compared with the trams themselves but it mattered not as they were mainly used during the night to clean the tracks of debris. National Tramway Museum, H.B. Priestley.

On 18 August 1946 Tram No.152, newly repainted and with enthusiasts 'hanging on', Bombay style, is positioned under the ex-Great Central Railway bridge at the junction of Abbey Park Road and Blackbird Road. The occasion was an early post-war tour of the system (still then largely complete) by the Light Railway Transport League. Its objective was the retention of tramways. Although thwarted by politicians determined to destroy this pollution-free transport, it is now a pressure group for the reinstatement of urban transit systems. The Leicester Co-operative Society Ltd (LCS Ltd) sold anything and everything and was a major retailer in the city and surrounding areas, paying a 'divvy' on purchases made. National Tramway Museum, J.E. Gready.

Tram No.178, the newest car in the fleet and still looking just that, despite having been in service for sixteen years by 1936 when this picture was taken at Narborough Road Terminus, awaits departure for the Clock Tower and on to Melton Road. With the upper deck windows fully opened, ladies hat fashions are clear, while on the lower deck the bowler hatted gentleman must surely be – a bank manager as well as a non-smoker! Directly underneath the word 'CITY' can be seen the additional braking system fitted to trams used on the Clarendon Park via Welford Road line.

The machine and armature workshops, located within the Abbey Park Road Depot, in 1930. The machinery was belt driven. This was skilled work and whatever the rate of pay it was a secure regular job, especially as the country was in the grips of the 'slump'. The 'old boy' working at the vice must be part of the fixtures and fittings!

'On Active Service', Leyland overhead repair wagon No.3 (BC 9909) with a fine body of men. The picture dates from the late 1920s and is a group photograph of the staff involved in the inspection and repair of the overhead wire, including the chief clerk (fifth from left) wearing a three piece suit with gold pocket watch at his waistcoat.

On a sunny day in 1950 the trackwork laid so thoroughly some 47 years earlier is being removed, with great difficulty! 'Hadsphaltic' were the contractors employed by the Corporation to make good the roadways after track removal within a half mile radius of the 'Clock Tower'. The roads were re-surfaced by hand and the labourers were reputed to be amongst the highest paid in the country. National Tramway Museum, A.W.V. Mace.

High Street, 1936. Lloyds Bank on the left and three immaculate trams. A schoolboy and his mother alight from Tram No.156, though it was not an official tram stop. Heading for Stoneygate, No.156 will 'keep right' into Gallowtree Gate where passengers would embark. Tram No.20, also advertising Nufix 'Dressing for the Hair', is about to leave the loading barrier for Fosse Road. Underneath Corts Ltd is the Irish Manufacturing Co, purveyors of linen goods, tablecloths and the like. The schoolboy would be over 80 years old by now and may well be still with us.

May 1938 and Humberstone Gate is full of immaculate trams. No.150 is on Route 8 to Coleman Road while the leading car is on Route 2, East Park Road. The large white building beyond is *The Bell Hotel*, once a coaching inn; Symingtons Coffee has long gone, although Schweppes soda water still mixes well with spirits! Ind Coope & Allsopp, famous for its bottled beers is no more, neither is Tram No.156 by-passing the central loading stand for Humberstone passengers heading towards the Clock Tower and on to Western Park, after loading passengers in the Haymarket. All the buildings have been demolished and the new Haymarket Centre has transformed the area; the road layout remains unaltered but nowadays is pedestrianised. National Tramway Museum, H.B. Priestley.

In May 1938 Tram No.50 leads a line of road vehicles past a request stop on Melton Road. The early Morris Commercial lorry is owned by Hawley & Johnson, dye merchants to the Leicester hosiery and knitwear industries. In the queue is a Morris 2 seater coupe of about 1927 while to the left a Vauxhall 14 awaits its opportunity to join the traffic after filling up with 'Shell' petrol.

On a bright summer's day in August 1949 Tram No.2 displaying 'Route 1 Belgrave' returns to the city centre from Stoneygate. At this location, approaching Victoria Park Road, the road vehicles are largely of pre-war manufacture; a Lanchester 10 hp motor car trails the tram while a Hillman Minx and van can be identified together with a 'Midland Red' single deck bus. Leicestershire Museums F.N.T., L.L. Jones.

At the top of London Road at Victoria Park Gates in May 1938, No.76 will shortly halt near to Mill Hill School to load and unload passengers before passing St James the Greater Church. On reaching Mayfield Corner it will turn right along Victoria Park Road and on to Clarendon Park. National Tramway Museum, H.B. Priestley.

In May 1937, Coronation time, three trams are decorated with bunting in High Street outside Lloyds Bank and the Loading Bay. No.177 is on Route 4 to Clarendon Park, while No.14 will veer left at the Clock Tower and on to Melton Road. Tram No.11 stands at the loading barrier outside Swears & Wells, furriers; the deviation of the trackwork in 1930 to accommodate this feature can be clearly seen. The Union Flag hangs on a pole from Lloyds – behind that upper storey window was, for many years, the spacious accommodation for the Bank Messenger. S.G. Jackman.

I have no idea how this happened in 1915, though playing at 'Dodgems' with the Corporation trams in the Depot yard was definitely not permitted... Whatever the cause, substantial damage was inflicted upon covered top car No.132 and an original open topper, No.67.

Belgrave Gate about 1908 with No.29, delivered in 1904 and displaying 'Melton Rd' notwithstanding that it is heading towards the Clock Tower. The Leicester Garage was an early enterprise and is merely a repair works. The tall round tower on the left is that of the 'Palace' Theatre. The area has now been redeveloped out of all recognition.

Horse tram No.27 in the 1890s on London Road.

An early view of a Leicester Corporation Tramways horse-drawn 'bus' taken in the 1880s. It is heading for Hinckley Road and the driver up top is well protected against the elements. The side advert is for F. Holland, a pianoforte retailer established in 1855. Smith was the clothier at 97 High Street.

Above, below and opposite. On Sunday 20 May 1943 this sequence was taken at the Stoneygate Terminus to illustrate the frequency of the service, even in wartime. The photographer, unusually, was an American serviceman, Mr G.F. Cunningham. The first shows No.129 (old livery) with 'Leicester' obliterated awaiting departure from the Terminus Time Clock. Shanklin Drive is to the left. The second has the next arrival, No.51 in new livery, with No.129 disappearing in the background. In the third, No.51 awaits departure, while No.16 has just arrived. The headlamps of all the trams have been modified to comply with wartime regulations. But the track continued to be well maintained – an essential as the trams provided 60% of all public transport services in the city. National Tramway Museum, G.F. Cunningham.

Newly overhauled Tram No.21 about to leave the Depot in Abbey Park Road on 16 July 1939 with an enthusiast's special for the Light Railway Transport League. The crew are no doubt wondering how they can take charge, as the enthusiasts have filled the loading platform! National Tramway Museum, W.A. Camwell.

On 21 September 1949 Tram No.80 emerges from 'The Hole in the Wall' next to *The Bell Hotel* in Humberstone Gate. The Leyland PDI bus No.251 entered service in 1946 and lasted a mere thirteen years whereas the tram, albeit modernised, was some 45 years old. The Tram Shelter reads 'Humberstone Cars', and was the central loading point for that route. National Tramway Museum, W.A. Camwell.

Two trams and two cars at Belgrave Terminus, 21 September 1938. No.97 is about to cross over to the line on which No.77 awaits departure to the Clock Tower and the clockwise East Park Road Route. Parked alongside is a Hillman Minx, on trade plates (02 BC) while a Morris 'Big Six' (JU 7985) squeezes past No.97 in the distance. National Tramway Museum, W.A. Camwell.

The old order changeth. In Humberstone Gate on 21 September 1949 Tram No.62 (advert-less!) awaits outside W.A. Lea & Son and the Charles Street Junction, outward bound to Humberstone, while No.138 approaches, crossing onto the single track and the shelter outside of Lewis'. The usurpers in the form of new Corporation buses – AEC Regent III No.54 and Leyland PD2 No.103 – are parked on the right and a 1938 Commer van, BJF 152, is negotiating a path between tram and bus delivering groceries for Worthingtons. All the cars are of pre-war manufacture; an Austin 10, Morris 12 and Hillman Minx are parked on the left. New cars were unavailable except for doctors and the like, as exports took priority. National Tramway Museum, W.A. Camwell.

No.83 in the Depot yard, 23 June 1937. One of those with extended frames and therefore a longer lower deck, it is in the immaculate condition customary for Leicester's public service vehicles. Two of the adverts are pertinent for products still popular seventy years on, Schweppes Ginger Ale and Kelloggs Corn Flakes (now salt reduced naturally!) The lorry just visible beyond belongs to J. Smith of Melbourne Road. National Tramway Museum, W.A. Camwell.

No.58 passing Belgrave Road station on 25 May 1938, heading towards the city centre and then route 2, East Park Road. The railway adverts are for cheap day excursions to various east coast destinations, while the Leicester Temperance Building Society exhorts passers-by to become their own homeowners (presumably teetotallers only!) National Tramway Museum, H.B. Priestley.

No.65 has reached the end of the line at the Coleman Road Terminus on 23 June 1937. On the road to the left is a 1933 Leyland TD3 diesel bus, going much further than the tram, to serve council housing estates built since the tram route opened in 1927. The tram shelter is the body from a withdrawn single deck bus. The ornate tram pole supports a solitary floodlight and the box attached to the pole itself housed a telephone for use by the tram crews in an emergency. The wooden fencing is beginning to fall into disrepair, as the line would close in 1938. National Tramway Museum, H.B. Priestley.

Tram No.156 basks in the sun on 23 June 1937 adjacent to Western Park Drive. The lower saloon destination blind has been altered to Belgrave Route No.1 and, hopefully, the conductor will alter the upper deck blinds before departure. The new Rover 12 hp was a vehicle much favoured by the upper middle classes as it had many refinements including a 'free wheel' device, positively lethal in today's traffic. Notwithstanding the latter-day demise of 'Rover' as a marque, it was always synonymous with quality. The large advert to the left is for a concert by *The Holwell Silver Band* at The De Montfort Hall Leicester, admission probably 1/- or 1/6d. The De Montfort Hall remains one of the finest concert halls in the country and has outstanding acoustics. Yet it was supposed to be a temporary structure when built in 1912! National Tramway Museum, H.B. Priestley.

Descending Welford Road towards Clarendon Park Tram No.104 is already displaying 'Depot' as its destination, for the line was to close later that day, 1 May 1945. A horse-cart (the rag and bone man's?) can just be seen on the left (Freeman's Common). The railings to the right border the Wyggeston Boys school playing fields. University Road is to the right at the summit of the hill and the tram poles still retain wartime white paint markings. R. Hubble, LCC Tramways Trust.

At Aylestone Terminus on 18 August 1946, newly painted No.152 has arrived with a Light Railway Transport League enthusiasts' special. The large poster proclaims 'The Tramway is the Modern Way', notwithstanding that politicians were determined to remove all trams from UK streets in favour of the all-conquering and polluting diesel bus. Worthington's the grocers can be seen on the left and behind the tram is a parade of shops owned by the Co-op. National Tramway Museum, J.E. Gready.

The days of electric trams are over but the 1924 Leyland Tower Wagon BC 9909 is still gainfully employed, parked on the pavement in Granby Street in the summer of 1950 as workmen remove overhead wire and supports from buildings to which they were attached. The vehicle was delivered with solid tyres and never modernised. The starting handle was essential as no self-starter was installed. An antique even in 1950, nowadays it would be a valuable vintage lorry.

BC 1078, the 1911 Leyland Tower Wagon, now 94 years old, has survived into preservation in the care of the Leicestershire Museum of Technology. It is depicted here in ordinary use, posed for the photographer in the depot yard at a late date, probably 1949. The mechanics of this vehicle are Edwardian and it is believed to be one of the oldest Leyland lorries in existence.

Coronation, May 1937. A quiet Humberstone Gate and Tram No.144, decorated for the occasion with the destination 'Western Park' Route No.1, is followed by a Midland Red single deck bus of about 1933. The policeman on 'point duty' is certainly doing that, especially as his toes are awkwardly pointing inwards. Every tram was so decorated that day and, as always, were immaculately turned out. Nearly seventy years later only Burtons Building on the right-hand corner survives. Lewis' magnificent Art Deco store, then but one year old has, apart from its famous tower, been demolished. The Haymarket Shopping Centre has replaced the many quality buildings and businesses shown here. S.G. Jackman.

It is wartime, 23 February 1943, but maintenance must go on to keep the trams running. No.143 is undergoing body repairs before being reunited with its Brill 21E truck. The paintwork is still in excellent order despite being some eight years old and if it was repainted at this time it would have been in the plain livery introduced in 1937. What is certain is that the quality of paint used would have been greatly inferior to that used in the mid-1930s. Jack Sills was a well known footwear retailer on Leicester Market. Peter Newland.

46

Eastgates and High Street beyond bustle with trams, motor vehicles and pedestrians on 24 January 1939. Tram No.146 in pre-1937 livery is turning from Gallowtree Gate on Route 1 heading for the loading barrier opposite Lloyds Bank and carries adverts for Hallams Coal and Typhoo Tea. Outside British Home Stores (selling wares priced from 3d to 5s) newly repainted Tram No.31 is heading for (eventually!) Groby Road, Route 9 via Belgrave Gate, Abbey Park Road, Blackbird Road and the Groby Road Terminus. The early 1930s lorry (a Bedford) belongs to Norman & Underwood Ltd., glaziers and lead merchants who are now internationally famous for restoring the windows and leadwork of historic buildings. Plate glass is still carried by lorries in a similar manner today.

The LMS station façade on London Road was and is a masterpiece by Charles Trubshaw and dates from 1892. The leading tram, No.21, has Route 3 Stoneygate as its destination while the following No.147 is on the East Park Road Route. Motor buses were introduced in 1924 and two early 1930s Corporation buses of Leyland manufacture carry the same livery as the trams. The LMS billboards advertise trips to London for 6/- (30p) and Glasgow. The Dove & Dove Leyland lorry and trailer is in sharp contrast to modern pantechnicons and would have been limited to a 20mph maximum speed by law. Whereas the trams lasted until 1949, the two buses had much shorter lives, being withdrawn in 1946. A.P. Newland.

At the Charles Street - Granby Street junction, the traffic lights are green as Tram No.151 heads towards the LMS station, with three Morris cars and a Wolseley following. All were manufactured between 1931 and 1936. Moreton's Café in Hotel Street was a favourite meeting place for shoppers for several decades. The vintage sports tourer parked by the pillar box, YS 5455, would be now much sought after by aficionados.

About 1943 Tram No.152 awaits departure from Narborough Road terminus back to the Clock Tower and on to Melton Road. The houses in the background still exist but the time clock and 'Cars Stop Here' sign most definitely do not. The tram still bears the legend CITY TRAMWAYS indicating that it was last repainted about 1934 and the paintwork is still very presentable. LEICESTER was deleted from every tram (and bus) as a wartime measure to bamboozle German invaders. The Bag Stores advert has no such inhibitions. W.J. Haynes.

On 18 August 1946 No.152, newly repainted, is on a tour of the system for members of the Light Rail Transport League. It was probably the only car to receive a post-war repaint. It is pictured in Fosse Road Central with a group of Light Rail Transport League enthusiasts, who appear to be mature gentlemen. National Tramway Museum.

Tram No.169 outside London Road station on 6 May 1943 exhorting the citizens to save rags, metal, paper bags etc for the war effort. National Tramway Museum.

The Clock Tower, festooned with Belisha beacons warning pedestrians to 'Mind How You Go' in April 1949. Tram No.178, not in the external condition of earlier days with only six months left, enters Humberstone Gate from Haymarket, destined for yet another circuit of the clockwise East Park Road circular route which closed on 15 May 1949. The new bus, an AEC Regent III bodied by Brush, entered service in March 1949, is on bus Route 31. National Tramway Museum.

On 24 April 1950 this act of vandalism took place. Tram No.36 is on its side having been separated from its Brill 21E truck and all electrical components. Set aside for preservation by Leicester City Transport for Leicester Museum on closure of the system, it was in the best overall condition and represented the final evolution of a Leicester Tram. Due to the usual 'in house' wrangling between Museum and Transport Department, no doubt on the question 'where shall we put it?' the Transport Department's patience ran out and it was broken up. On 25 April 1950 – the following day – the Museum reached agreement and asked for the tram to be handed over... If it had not been for the foresight of enthusiasts who located No.76 in Yorkshire and raised £100 to save it and take it to Crich, no Leicester tram would have been rescued for posterity. Leicester Mercury.

At the junction of Uppingham Road and Victoria Road East, Tram No.133 in sparkling condition, has 'Clarendon Park' as destination. Goodess – a chemist – is selling potions at 'town prices' while next door a tobacconist advertises Player's Navy Cut cigarettes and Fry's chocolate. The scene is a very peaceful one and the group of boys gathered around the lamp post island are certainly not causing any mischief. National Tramway Museum.

In this view of Belgrave Gate dating from about 1923 Tram No.56, in its original open top condition, is heading towards the Clock Tower and then East Park Road. The following tram has been partially modernised by the fitting of an enclosed upper deck roof. Apart from the horse and dray, the only other road vehicle is a very early open top double deck bus. Leicester Corporation took delivery of six Tilling Stevens single deck buses in 1924 but the vehicle in this picture is not one of them. It must belong to an unknown small independent local operator. The awning to the left is that of the *Palace Theatre*, an entertainment 'Mecca' before the days of radio and television. The whole of this run-down part of the city was cleared for widening and track renewal in the late 1920s and the scene nowadays is unrecognisable. Peter Newland.

Clarendon Park/Queens Road corner in the last winter of tramway operation, 1948/49. Tram No.75, a rebuild with extended frames, is about to turn into Queens Road and head towards the city centre and thence Blackbird Road. L.A. Burbidge & Co was nominally a cycle repair shop, but to boys was more importantly a stockist of Hornby Trains, Meccano and Dinky Toys, all in very short supply – so much so that there was a waiting list for the latest models! J. Copping was the gent's hairdresser and tobacconist, remembered for giving boys a very short back and sides for a reasonable price. The two identifiable cars following the tram are both British. AKV 384 is a 1936 Morris 8 fitted with a radiator muff to keep the engine warm, while just visible is a 1934 Morris 10. The young man on his bike has all-weather gear, cape and leggings tied to a carrier behind the saddle. Today all the buildings survive but shop ownership and uses have changed of course. The trams ceased on 15 March 1949 but it is a fair bet that the track is still there under layers of tarmac. National Tramway Museum.

On one of the final days of operation on the Clarendon Park route, Tram No.83 passes W.T. Hind, the chemist. Parked outside is Mr Hinds' Wolseley 18hp dating from 1938 and if memory serves it was painted in a two-tone grey; certainly it was a luxurious vehicle. The tram has received a lick of paint by the look of it. 'Potions and cure-alls' from a bye-gone age can be identified in the window adverts. This chemist was also a wine and spirit merchant (!) and Sandemans wine and port and Gilbey wines and spirits were available. National Tramway Museum.

Tram No.92 in East Park Road, where there were several familiar Leicester factories, in March 1949. The Art Deco style building on the left is that of 'Chilprufe', once well-known for children's clothing while beyond was the factory belonging to Imperial Typewriters Ltd. National Tramway Museum.

A passing loop at the junction of Clarendon Park Road and St Leonards Road in March 1949 with Tram No.7 passing No.93. The latter is heading towards the terminus in Welford Road. The trackwork looks past its best but would only be required for a few more days as the route closed on 15 March 1949. 'Worthingtons', once 'the grocer that fed you', has long gone. Leicestershire Museums F.N.T., L.L. Jones.

Tram No.94, equipped with 'slipper brakes', in the summer of 1936 at the summit of Cemetery Hill (gravestones on the right) on Welford Road heading towards the Clarendon Park terminus. Passengers on this trip were few and far between and the service infrequent. The route closed on 1 May 1945 when victory in Europe was assured. S. Newton.

Tram No.100 in 1935, in spotless condition, picking up numerous passengers outside chemist F.H. Clark, in Humberstone Gate. Its destination, East Park Road Route 2, is clear enough and confirmed by the side destination blind in the lower saloon, emphasising that it is 'via Humberstone Road'. Outside the Transport Department enquiry office is a motor cycle-sidecar combination and a 1930 Austin 'Heavy 12'. Nothing in this picture now exists, for all has been replaced by the new 'Haymarket Centre'. National Tramway Museum.

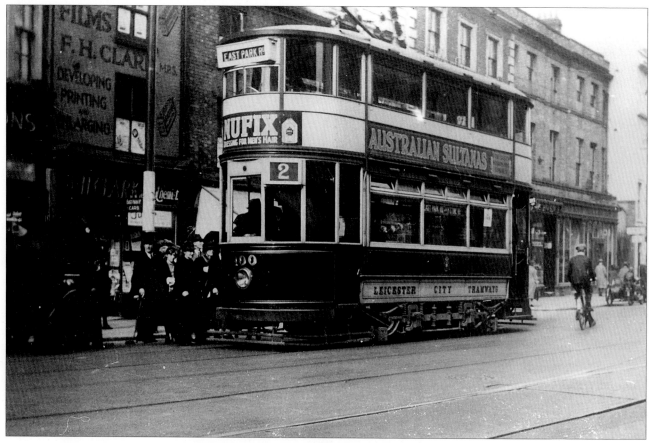

In late 1937 Tram No.125 leans on the curve to the Coleman Road Terminus which was on a short section of reserved track; it was the last route to open (in 1927) and the second to close, in October 1938. On the railway bridge parapet is an advert for McDougalls Self Raising Flour. The 1950s TV advert declared that it was 'the flour which never varies'! S. Newton.

Emerging from the 'Hole in the Wall' next to the *Bell Hotel* on its final journey to the Abbey Park Road Depot in Humberstone Gate, 9 November 1949, is the last tram, No.58 fully loaded with VIPs. The new AEC Regent III bus will take over the duties performed so well by the trams for over 45 years. A contemporary report states that the horns of all buses parked in Humberstone Gate sounded a raucous tribute to 'the old lady of the lines'. Leicester Mercury.

Tram No.86 was experimentally rebuilt in 1923 at great expense. It was relatively expensive because the rest of the fleet were 'modernised' simply by enclosing the open balconies with glass and steel sheeting. Thus no other trams were reconstructed like it and its distinctive appearance amongst a large fleet of standard trams marked it out for over twenty-five years. Still in its original ornate livery but carrying the legend LEICESTER CITY TRANSPORT the period is the summer of 1935. It is outside the then *Freemens Arms*, opposite the Granby Halls, returning from Aylestone to Horsefair Street, Route 5. National Tramway Museum.

Tram No.129 halts outside Lloyds in High Street, the bank flying a banner exhorting its customers to spend less on themselves and invest in 'Savings Bonds'. Behind are a 1936 Morris 10 and a Bedford van of similar vintage owned by the 'Coalville Last Co Ltd'. No.129 will depart from a limited stop and resume its journey to Stoneygate. Visible on the lamp post outside Gilbey's is a direction sign for an Air Raid Shelter... It is a quiet Sunday, 20 May 1943. National Tramway Museum, G.F. Cunningham.

On a bright day in the summer of 1949, Trams No.80 and No.7 are pictured at Humberstone Terminus. The conductor walks to the Gledhill time clock with his waybill to record the time of departure. No.80 will depart for the city centre and No.7 will follow a few minutes later. External condition is not so pristine as in the past – their days were numbered and three months later they would run no more. A.D. Packer.

On 10 August 1947 No.86 was hired by a group of enthusiasts to tour the system. Standing by the driver is (it is believed) Mr L.H. Smith, later to become the General Manager of Leicester City Transport. The 1937 Morris 10 probably belonged to Mr Smith as roadside parking was normally prohibited. The station hoardings are still lettered LMS of course and the smiling couple on the large advertisement have clearly taken their daily dose of 'Andrews Liver Salts', keeping them healthy!

Before the installation of route numbers and when Clarendon Park was a circular route ending at Aylestone, a modernised No.87 travels along Victoria Park Road towards London Road. The tracks are laid, curiously, to one side with only room for cyclists on the nearside. A trilby hatted cyclist opts to use the walkway. The sole car, XG 518, is a 1931 Austin 'Harley' saloon registered in the West Riding of Yorkshire. Leicester Mercury.

Tram No.88 stands outside the Art Deco tram shelter, one of several built by the Corporation in the mid-1930s, on 7 July 1937. Humberstone Terminus is the location and the Trocadero Cinema can be seen in the distance. BXP989, a 1935 registered Morris 8, is parked against the kerb and to the right a policeman's bike rests against a Leicester City Police hut; no doubt the duty 'bobby' is reporting in. National Tramway Museum, W.A. Camwell.

On a miserable January day in 1939, trams are in abundance in High Street. No.100 is loading passengers for Narborough Road Route 2; No.90 has been repainted and overhauled and is passing T. Foster & Co and W.A. Gilbey & Co, both wine and spirit merchants. Manners was the shop for school uniforms. The tram has come from Blackbird Road and will turn right into Gallowtree Gate and south to Clarendon Park. Another tram No.106 (they did come together – at times) in the old livery is outside Lloyds Bank. A motley collection of motor vehicles stretches past the window of J. Grice & Sons. Peter Newland.

The legendary Henry Priestley, who devoted much of his time, including his honeymoon, to photographing provincial tram systems, took this picture in May 1938. It shows Belgrave Road and the LNER (ex-Great Northern) station. Tram No.92, fully loaded, is held up by sheep ahead, presumably being walked from the station cattle dock to an abattoir. Corrigan footwear on the corner has a wonderful hanging display – they also sold shoes in Leicester Market. The cycles are real period pieces and the London North Eastern Railway adverts exhort locals to visit Hull for 6/3d (30½p) or, a much better prospect, Bridlington for 7/9d. LNER also stood (unfairly) for the Late and Never Early Railway! Ovaltine, Heinz Salad Cream and Bovril (reformulated) are still with us, but demand for Stephen's ink has somewhat dried up. All the buildings to the left and the railway station to the right are no more. The Belgrave area has been transformed by Asian immigrants who have made their home in Leicester, a place now acclaimed for its ethnic cuisine. National Tramway Museum, H.B. Priestley.

No.119, somewhat scarred, waits while passengers board at the rear entrance on 26 May 1947 at Victoria Park Gate. Typhoo Tea still quenches our thirsts. Entering the picture going to either Clarendon Park or Stoneygate is No.16. The imposing buildings in the background still exist, although Mill Hill School behind No.119 has long closed. Leicestershire Museums F.N.T., L.L. Jones.

Although the sign in front of the Clock Tower clearly states 'Keep Left' the trams did not obey the rule as can be seen in this view taken from Haymarket in early 1936. Tram No.125 is heading for Blackbird Road on Route 4 past *The Eclipse* which emphatically proclaims 'Shipstones Only' as the beer available. A much-lamented brew indeed, is 'Shippo'. Between the two trams is Berry's poultry shop with an array of birds in the window 'hanging'. They were, comparatively, a luxury food then. Both cars were manufactured by Morris Motors at Cowley, Oxford, where BMW 'Minis' are now produced. JU3431 is a Morris 10 registered in December 1933 while the car avoiding the tram and cyclists is a Morris Cowley dating from 1928. Leicester Mercury.

On 25 May 1938 No.136 is at the Melton Road Terminus, probably on its first revenue earning trip after overhaul and repainting. A Ford 8, the first £100 saloon car, is partially obscured by the lamp post and tram pole, while a 1936 Morris 8 JU 8891, a much superior car with hydraulic brakes, overtakes. Hayley's Garage on the right is spick and span selling a range of petrols including 'National Benzole' once distilled from coal by British Colliers. The Garage offered washing and greasing with 'super all-electric equipment.' Castrol oil was dispensed from bulk into a can with a spout for the motorist to top up the engine oil level of his car in the days when oil consumption was a problem. Using the crossover and automatic trolley pole reverser, No.136 will reverse to the city-bound track and its journey will take it to the Clock Tower, Humberstone Road and on to East Park Road. This idyllic scene is no more, swamped by urban and commercial development. Henry Priestley, a schoolmaster by profession, specialised in photographing every provincial tramway in the UK before the Second World War. He and his contemporary, W.A. Camwell, were largely responsible for recording for posterity tramways at their peak, before the neglect of World War Two hastened their demise. National Tramway Museum, H.B. Priestley.

On a wet day in September 1938, newly overhauled No.3 waits at the Town Hall Terminus in Bowling Green Street for departure to Aylestone. The conductor is maybe having a last minute 'fag' before commencing duty. The advert on the tram stop is for Leicester's annual 'Home Life Exhibition' held in the Granby Halls, now sadly demolished and the site a car park for the Leicester Royal Infirmary. The open car MW 4544 with a 'dicky' seat is probably a Morris 'Cowley' and, being at least ten years old, was no doubt some young man's first car – the passenger (Dad?) is holding on for dear life! D.R. Harvey.

Tram No.123, newly fitted with a canopy top and posed outside the Depot together with its driver and conductor in 1913. It was probably the first 'open topper' to be so treated, as all the other trams were still 'topless'. The lower deck destination blinds are quite ornate in describing the route. Henry Hart & Son was a progressive enterprise holding 'an immense stock' and importantly were *on the phone*. An advert for Hudson's Soap can just be discerned above the conductor. 'Gossages' was another soap product of the period. National Tramway Museum.

In high summer 1948 Tram No.7 has been halted at the Victoria Park gates, to pick up more fare-paying passengers. The standard bamboo trolley pole can be seen attached to the lower deck bodywork, under the lines of rivets. It was useful if the roof trolley current collector became unhooked though this was a rare occurrence. No motorised traffic is in sight – there was literally no petrol other than for essential users and then only with a Ministry of Fuel permit! National Tramway Museum.

Tram No.20 turning from the Haymarket into Humberstone Gate to take up service on Route 1 – East Park Road via Humberstone Road. The car in front is a Ford of American design dating from 1935. Burton's 'The Tailor' occupies the Art Deco building. Incredibly there were three Burton shops around the Clock Tower. Wand's Chemists, the cash drug dispensary, had a chain of outlets throughout the city and were taken over by Timothy Whites & Taylors immediately after the war. D.R. Harvey.

On a cold winter Sunday in 1947 No.26 has halted at the tram stop to load/unload passengers, before turning right into Victoria Park Road and on to Clarendon Park. The permanent way and setts are still well cared for, though the route would close some two years later. The impressive building is St James the Greater Church, modelled on Torcello Cathedral in Venice. Other than passengers on No.26 and two pedestrians, there is little sign of life; maybe it was 'Matins' at 11 o'clock. National Tramway Museum.

P60 1643

Outward	FARE	Inward
1st Stage	**1d**	1st Stage
2nd Stage		2nd Stage
3rd Stage		3rd Sta.
4th Stage		4th Stage
Ter-minus		Centre

E 3233

CITY OF LEICESTER TRAMWAYS & MOTOR OMNIBUS DEPARTMENT

Special Night Service

CHILD'S FARE . 3d

This ticket is avail-able as a Through Fare or Transfer, on any Two Routes. Passengers transfer-ring to connecting Route must retain this Ticket for the Second Stage. To be given up for an Exchange Ticket.

D 2063

CITY OF LEICESTER TRAMWAYS & MOTOR OMNIBUS DEPARTMENT

LATE PASSENGER SERVICE

CHILD'S FARE 3d

OUTWARD		INWARD
Terminus		Centre

City of Leicester Tramways & Motor Omnibus Department

LATE PASSENGER SERVICE

CHILDS FARE **3d**

Available only on date for which issued For One Journey Only. To be given up to the Conductor in lieu of fare

Not Transferable

A 0814

B 8387

CITY OF LEICESTER TRAMWAYS & MOTOR OMNIBUS DEPARTMENT

LATE PASSENGER SERVICE

FOR CHILDS 3d. TICKET

| Terminus | EXCHANGE | Centre |

City of Leicester Tramways & Motor Omnibus Department

SPECIAL LATE PASSENGER SERVICE

Fare 1/-

Available only on date for which issued For One Journey Only. To be given up to the Conductor in lieu of Fare Not Transferable.

0 0935

B99 1150

Outward	FARE	Inward
1st Stage	**1½d**	1st Stage
2nd Stage		2nd Stage
		Horse-fair Street
Terminus		Clock Tower

City of Leicester Passenger Transport Department

LATE PASSENGER SERVICE

CHILD'S FARE **3d.**

Available only on date for which issued. For One Journey Only. To be given up to the Conductor in lieu of Fare Not Transferable.

E 2021

0 6621

City of Leicester Passenger Transport Department

Special Night Service

Fare - 6d

This ticket is avail-able as a Through Fare or Transfer, on any Two Routes. Passengers transfer-ring to connecting Route must retain this Ticket for the Second Stage. To be given up for an Exchange Ticket.

Colleys, Printers, London

LEICESTER CITY TRANSPORT

½d. Child's Ticket

Available on any ½d Stage. Must be given in exchange for ordinary ticket

General Manager & Engineer

NE 2447

LEICESTER CITY TRANSPORT

1½d Prepaid Ticket

Available on any 1½d Stage. MUST BE GIVEN IN EXCHANGE FOR ORDINARY TICKET.

General Manager & Engineer.

ML 00246

LEICESTER CITY TRANSPORT

3d PREPAID TICKET

Available on any 3d STAGE Must be given in exchange for Ordinary Ticket.

General Manager

U 7179

W 0266

City of Leicester Passenger Transport Department.

LATE PASSENGER SERVICE

| Terminus | FOR 6d TICKET EXCHANGE | Centre |

Colleys, Printers, London

Y 8844

LEICESTER CITY TRANSPORT

LATE PASSENGER SERVICE

Fare 6d

Available only on vehicle on which issued and to sta-tion punched, for one journey only. Not Transferable

Williamson, Printer, Ashton

Leicester City Transport.

LATE PASSENGER SERVICE

Fare 6d.

Available only on date for which issued. For One Journey Only. To be given up to the Conductor in lieu of Fare Not Transfe able.

Cb 5751

L92 5619

Leicester City Transport Issued subject to Bye-laws. Available only on vehicle on which issued to station punched. To be given up on demand.

OUT		IN
1	**1d**	1
2	CHILDS	2
3		3
4		4
5	STAGE	5

Williamson, Printer, Ashton

69U 0327

	STAGE FARE	
1		1
2	**1½d**	2
3		3
4		4
5		5
6		6
7		7
8		8

F91 5960

OUTWARD STAGES	STAGE FARE	INWARD STAGES
1		1
2	**2d**	2
3		3
4		4
5		5
6		6

Leicester City Transport

C 9378

Special Night Service

CHILD'S FARE **4d**

This ticket is avail-able as a Through Fare or Transfer on any Two Routes. Passengers transfer-ring to connecting Route must retain this Ticket for the Second Stage. To be given up for an Exchange Ticket.

Williamson, Printer, Ashton